DON'T SAY THAT!

LET'S TALK NICELY

By Janine Amos and Annabel Spenceley
Consultant Rachael Underwood

Published in the United States by Windmill Books (Alphabet Soup)
Windmill Books
303 Park Avenue South
Suite #1280
New York, NY 10010-3657

U.S. publication copyright ©Evans Brothers Limited 2009
First North American Edition

Library of Congress Cataloging-in-Publication Data

Amos, Janine
      Don't say that! : let's talk nicely / by Janine Amos and Annabel Spenceley.
           p.   cm. – (Best behavior)
      Contents: Painting animals—Making Jello.
      Summary: Two brief stories demonstrate the importance of avoiding mocking
and careless speech when we speak to one another.
      ISBN 978-1-60754-031-1 (lib.) – 978-1-60754-054-0 (pbk.)
978-1-60754-055-7 (6 pack)
      1. Interpersonal communication—Juvenile literature   2. Etiquette for children and
teenagers—Juvenile literature [1. Behavior 2. Etiquette 3. Conduct of life] I. Spenceley,
Annabel II. Title III. Series
      177'.1—dc22

American Library Binding 13-digit ISBN: 978-1-60754-031-1
Paperback 13-digit ISBN: 978-1-60754-054-0
6 pack 13-Digit ISBN: 978-1-60754-055-7

Manufactured in China

Credits:
Editor: Louise John
Designer: D.R. Ink
Photography: Gareth Boden
Production: Jenny Mulvanney

With thanks to our models:
Chaitun Bagary, Kai Walden, Holly Walker-Spring, and Georgia and Rebecca Britton.

Painting Animals

Everyone is painting animal pictures.

Chaitun paints a dog. He paints very carefully.

Kai paints a dog, too. He splashes paint all over his picture.

Kai points at
Chaitun's picture.

"That's not a dog!" he laughs.

"Don't say that!" shouts Chaitun.

"You can't paint a dog!"
laughs Kai.

Chaitun throws
down his brush.

**How do you think
Chaitun feels?**

Julia comes over. "Stop it, Chaitun! It's not OK to hit. Let's talk about it."

"He says my painting isn't a dog!" says Chaitun.

"It's not OK to say that, Kai," explains Julia. "Chaitun feels upset."

"You painted your dog your way," says Julia. "Chaitun painted his dog his way."

"Let's look at all the paintings," says Julia.

"They are all very different!" says Kai. "Yes," smiles Julia. "Everyone has very different ideas!"

Making Jello

Rebecca has made cups of Jello for her birthday party later.

"Are they ready now? Can I get them out?" she asks.

"Let's have a look," says Mom.

"Some are ready," she smiles. "We can start to take them out."

Rebecca feels excited. She starts to turn them out onto a plate.

She turns out more and more.

"Whoa! Stop!" says Mom. "Those green ones aren't ready yet!"

"Oh, I'm stupid!" sighs Rebecca.

"Don't say that!" says Mom. "It's not true, you just made a mistake."

"But what can we do with the green ones now?" asks Rebecca.

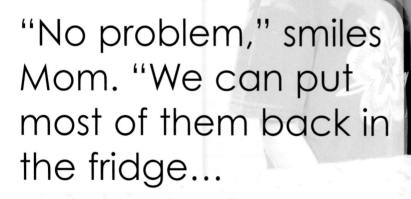

"No problem," smiles Mom. "We can put most of them back in the fridge...

and get them
out later!"

FOR FURTHER READING

INFORMATION BOOKS

Krasny Brown, Laurie. *How to Be a Friend: a Guide to Making Friends and Keeping Them.* Boston: Little, Brown Young Readers, 2001.

FICTION

Grindley, Sally. *The Big What Are Friends For? Storybook.* New York: Kingfisher, 2002.

Morris, Jennifer. *May I Please Have a Cookie? (Scholastic Reader).* New York: Cartwheel Books, 2005.

AUTHOR BIO

Janine has worked in publishing as an editor and author, as a lecturer in education. Her interests are in personal growth and raising self-esteem and she works with educators, child psychologists and specialists in mediation. She has written more than fifty books for children. Many of her titles deal with first time experiences and emotional health issues such as Bullying, Death, and Divorce.

You can find more great fiction and nonfiction from Windmill Books at windmillbks.com